Mary Queen of the Scots
The Forgotten Reign

By Laurel A. Rockefeller

Mary Queen of the Scots is a work of narrative history based on events in the life of Queen Mary Stuart and constructed using primary and secondary historical sources, commentary, and research.

Consulted sources appear at the end of this book. Interpretation of source material is at the author's discretion and utilized within the scope of the author's imagination, including names, events, and historical details.

Love this book? Share the love of this book by kindly reviewing this book on your blog, website, and on major retailer websites. Your review not only offers this author your feedback for improvement of this book series, but helps other people find this book so they can enjoy it as well. Only a few sentences and a few minutes of your time is all it takes to share the love with those who want to enjoy it too.

Copyright © 2015 Laurel A. Rockefeller
All rights reserved.
ISBN: 1511929839
ISBN-13: 978-1511929837

Laurel A. Rockefeller

Table of Contents

OF SCOTLAND FORGOTTEN 4
CHAPTER ONE: PARIS 5
CHAPTER TWO: RETURN TO SCOTLAND 13
CHAPTER THREE: QUEEN MARY MUST REMARRY 28
CHAPTER FOUR: MURDER IN HOLYROOD 41
CHAPTER FIVE: LOSS OF THE THRONE 51
TIMELINE 58
PRAYERS IN LATIN AND THEIR TRANSLATIONS 66
SONG LYRICS FROM MARY QUEEN OF THE SCOTS 68
SUGGESTED READING 71

Of Scotland Forgotten

Woe to thee, oh Scotland
Our Pictish mothers' tears like highland rain
For the queens of old are forgotten
Their valour now seen as depraved.
Where is your love for your queens
For Picts and Scots, Gaels and Brigantes?
For fair Mary your queen -- cast aside
And praised instead the Puritan's hateful hand.
You drove the fairest queen far away
To die disgraced on an English axe
Spilling the fairest and most Scottish blood of all.
And with her died the Scottish heart: brave and free.

Chapter One: Paris

"The king is dead! Long live the queen!" cried the herald. Lights and sounds blurred together as the five year-old Mary stirred from her sleep. Was it a memory or just a dream?

Rising from her bed Mary patiently took still as servants dressed her in a miniature version of one of the gowns her mother and regent wore, "Where is mama?"

"In her office," replied one servant as she pulled on the queen's over-gown and laced it up in back.

"I want to see mama!"

"I am sorry Your Majesty but you will not see her for a very long time."

"Why?"

"Today we are taking you to Leith harbour where you will board a ship bound for France."

"Why?"

"Many reasons."

"Tell me."

"To keep you safe, to make sure nobles who do not like your mother cannot use you to hurt the country."

"There's something else, isn't there?"

"Before he died last year, your great uncle King Henry the Eighth of England wanted you to marry his son Prince Edward. Now that Edward is king of England, there are many who are more determined than ever that you should marry him and unite the realms of Scotland and England in the process."

"Why is that bad?"

"Well to start with, England has always been our enemy."

"Always?"

"Sadly yes."

"Why?"

"Well because for as long as people have written down history the English have tried to conquer our peoples. They invade and we fight back to defend ourselves. Sometimes we have invaded England too to make our kingdom bigger or to make it safer against the English. To make things even more confusing, there are many nobles from England who own land in Scotland and many Scots who own land in England; the division between our kingdoms has never been all that clear. That is another reason why we are at war so much. Where does England stop and Scotland begin? Sometimes that depends on the day!" explained the servant.

"But if I marry King Edward, maybe the fighting will stop! Maybe it would be good to live in England."

"That is not what your mother wants."

"Well maybe my mother does not know everything. I am queen!"

"Yes you are queen; you are also five years old! It is very naughty for you to want to disobey her! That is a sin, Mary."

"Is sin bad?"

"Very bad! You do not want to spend eternity in hell do you?"

"What is hell?"

"A very bad place. I am not a priest though; I am only a woman and cannot teach you about these things."

"You sound as if being a woman is bad."

"Yes, it is very bad, Your Majesty. God made men better than us. We are weak and do bad things because we are weak. But you must speak to a priest. There will be one on the ship to France you can talk to."

"Will I be the only Scottish lass in France?"

"No, of course not. Many girls are coming with you, sent to Scotland by their parents to protect them."

"Protect them from what?"

"Bad people who want to do bad things."
"Here in Scotland?"
"Yes."
"Who?!"
"Your Majesty, we must go!"
"I don't want to go!"
"Your Majesty, please!"

Mary paced and pouted, jumping up and down in a tantrum. Finally after letting out her emotions a little she eyed the servant, "I still do not want to go."

"Will you come with me now?"
"Yes."
"Thank you Your Majesty."

Two hours later Queen Mary found herself walking up the ramp to the beautiful sailing shipped moored in Leith harbour in Edinburgh. Running playfully around the top deck she spotted four girls, all of them also named Mary, playing hide and seek. Queen Mary ran up to them, "Can I play too?"

"Who are you?" asked Mary Seton.
"I'm the queen!"
"You are not!" giggled Mary Fleming.
"Yes I am," asserted Queen Mary.

"Yes you are," affirmed the queen's half-brother Lord James Stewart. Kneeling he kissed the queen's hand, "I am forever at Your Majesty's service."

"Who are you?" asked Queen Mary.

"James Stewart."

"My last name is Stewart too! Are we related?"

James laughed, "I am your brother!"

"If you are my brother, why are you not king?"

"Because Queen Mary of Guise is not my mother."

"I do not understand."

"You will, my queen!"

"Is your mother alive?"

"Very much so. She wants me to tell you that she prays every day for your majesty's health."

"Does my mother know your mother?"

"Yes."

"Does she know you?"

"Yes."

"How old are you?"

"Seventeen."

"I am only five."

"You were born just a few days before our father the king died, God rest his soul."

"Are you coming to France with us?"

"For a little while, yes. That is if you don't mind having a brother." Queen Mary opened her arms. James hugged her tightly and kissed her cheek, "Everything will be okay, Your Majesty."

"Call me Mary; we are family!"

"Depairte, depairte, allace I most depairte. From hir that hes my hairt with hairt full soir; again's my in deid and can find no remeid, I wait the pan's of deid can do no moir!" sang the ten year old Queen Mary as she played her lute, the Scottish lyrics of the song feeling oddly alien after five years in Paris.

"Marie! Marie! News from London!" cried Prince François excitedly.

"Quelles nouvelles?" asked Queen Mary in French.

"Your cousin, King Edward the Sixth!"

"What about him?" puzzled Mary.

"He's dead! He died of consumption three weeks ago."

Mary crossed herself, "Poor lad!"

"There is more, ma chérie. Your cousin Lady Jane Grey, granddaughter of your great aunt Mary and the duke of Suffolk Charles

Brandon, she is now imprisoned in the Tower of London!"

"For what crime?"

"The king tried to override his father's last will and testament by making her queen instead of Queen Mary. For nine days she ruled as Queen Jane before the queen and her sister the Lady Elizabeth entered London to claim the throne officially. As soon as Queen Mary arrived, all support for Queen Jane disappeared."

"The people have spoken! Let us pray that through the wisdom of Queen Mary we might see England restored to the true religion."

François crossed himself, "In nómine Patris et Fílii et Spíritus Sancti. Amen."

"Amen," echoed Mary with a playful smile as she kissed his cheek. Grinning, François took her hand and kissed it.

Paris glittered excitedly as King Henri the Second, Queen Catherine de Medici, princes and princesses, cardinals, bishops, the queen's half-brother Lord James Stewart, and all manner of nobles gathered for the long awaited wedding of

Queen Mary to Prince François at Cathédrale Notre-Dame de Paris. Now fifteen, Queen Mary dazzled the crème de la crème of French society in her brilliant white wedding gown with its royal train. Two girls walked behind the queen, carrying her long train and helping her navigate its luxurious volume. The most beautiful diamond necklace in all of 16th century France adorned the angelic teenaged queen. A golden coronet rested gracefully on her brow. Yet for all the sparkle and glamour of these, nothing compared to the joy bubbling within Queen Mary's heart as she said her vows to François and became his wife. It was a moment she would never forget; a moment doomed to yield to sorrow, pain, and death.

Chapter Two: Return to Scotland

"En mon triste et doux chant. D'un ton fort lamentable, je jette un oeil trenchant de perte incomparable, et en soupirs cuisants passe mes meilleurs ans," wrote Queen Mary, her tears flowing freely as she tried to express her sorrow. "My dearest love! How will I ever live without you? François! François! Why did you leave me? How could you be so cruel, sweetheart? First ma mère dies and now you so soon after! Oh Mary mother of God! Please, please, I beg you! Help me! I am too young to be a widow!"

Hearing her queen's cries of heart-felt agony, Mary Seton rushed to her, kneeling, the queen's tears bringing tears to her own eyes, "Ma reine! I swear it will be alright! You are loved here in Paris!"

"Paris! Can it be my home any longer?"

Mary Seton embraced her queen and friend, "It would be if not for your mother in law."

"Oui, c'est ça," admitted Queen Mary. "I do not begrudge King Louis his crown; I did not bear François a son, there was no time! But

Queen Catherine de Medici; she is wrong to hate me just because her husband loved me! Are all mothers in law so cruel to their son's wives?"

"Not that I have seen," observed Mary Seton. "But then again, we are all so young! Do you ever wonder if our mothers were right to send us to France as little girls?"

"King Henri the Second loved me, Mary, of that I am certain. I grew up with François knowing that when we were old enough we were going to marry. François loved me dearly and I loved him! No, Marie, I have no regrets. Besides, moving to Paris ensured no one was going to marry me off to anyone in London— least of all that heretic King Edward the Sixth!"

"A great blessing! I heard your cousin the king was a far greater heretic than his father! King Henry the Eighth it is said kept the true religion in his heart and only broke away from Rome so he could marry that witch Anne Boleyn. But his son King Edward—he truly believed in the heresies!"

"Of all the English heretics, Edward the Sixth was the worst! May he suffer eternity in hell for his crimes against the faithful! Queen Mary tried to bring England back; now she is gone and her bastard sister sits the throne!"

"Ma reine, you must go to London and take the throne from Elizabeth! You are Queen Mary's only legal heir!" pleaded Mary Seton.

"If I go to London to claim the throne, Queen Elizabeth will certainly kill me," observed Queen Mary.

"Then we will go home to Edinburgh! You are Scotland's queen. It is time to rule as queen."

"Yes … you are right. After thirteen years in France, it is time to go home!"

Returning to Scotland proved difficult and dangerous. Together the wind, tides, currents, and rocky shallows of the English Channel seemed determined to sink Queen Mary's small ship. Below decks Queen Mary prayed for the safety of all on board. On deck, her dedicated crew battled the elements; carefully navigating to avoid Queen Elizabeth's waiting fleet by sailing nearly twenty miles from the shore. Finally after five days and nights the shores of Leith harbour in Edinburgh greeted them to much rejoicing and relief.

"James! C'est toi?" asked Queen Mary as she stepped off the ramp from her ship.

Smiling Lord James Stewart bowed deeply, kissing her hand, "It is a great pleasure to see you again, my queen!"

Queen Mary wrapped her arms around him in a warm hug, "I am so blessed you are the first to see me returned from France!"

"We are family!"

"How is your mother?"

"She is well, thank you for asking. How are you feeling? When I heard about your mother, my heart ached for you. We disagreed about religion, but she was a good ruler and she genuinely believed in me for which I owe her a great deal."

"You knew her better than I," confessed Mary.

"Would you trade away one moment of your time in Paris?"

"Mais non! Je—"

James brushed away the tears forming on the edges of Mary's eyes, "You were so beautiful at your wedding, Mary. Your love for him really showed."

"Pardonnez-moi. It is not becoming a queen to cry so easily."

"Yes it is when the queen has lost her one true love," reassured James.

"Do you think I will ever love like that again?"

"I cannot say. But if there is a way for you to find love again, it most certainly will come to you."

"Merci beaucoup mon frère!"

"De rien," smiled James. "Now if you are done with life at sea may I suggest we return to the palace? A grand party is waiting for you full of music, feasting, and dancing at Holyrood."

Queen Mary took his arm as he led her to her carriage and opened the door for her, "Merci."

Music flooded the banqueting hall in Holyrood. As Queen Mary entered the spacious room she felt all eyes upon her. A steward handed the queen a finely crafted silver cup filled with French wine. Mary took a sip, "Merci beaucoup." Sitting down at the high table Queen Mary was delighted to see a fashionable selection of forks set to the left of her gilded silver plate. Servants brought Queen Mary a dazzling selection of fish, lobster, chicken, beef, mutton, and pork which she sampled eagerly, keeping the portions of each small in accord with tradition. Fine white bread and hearty rye bread sopped up the sauces and countered the taste of the strong spices that seasoned the meat. Honey butter waited in a dish on her right for when she wished to sweeten her bread. For dessert she found marzipan shaped like the French fleur-de-lys, pears richly baked in cinnamon and honey, and French tarts seasoned with expensive vanilla.

As Queen Mary nibbled at her desserts, Lord James approached her with a bow, "Would you care to dance, Your Majesty?" Smiling Queen Mary took his hand as he graciously led her to the nearby dance floor. Following French custom, the dancing opened with a series of bransles including Bransle de l'Official, Bransle les Lavandieres, and Bransle de Chevaulx before changing over to more regal pavane dances popular in European royal courts. "You dance very well, Your Majesty."

"I love dancing—and singing. Or rather I used to love these things."

"You will again. The heart heals and you are both strong and beautiful. Give it time. Until then, perhaps you will find comfort by focusing on getting to know your people again. A new parliament will need to be called soon."

Offer ID: 296152
Price Paid: 0.83

Very Good
Jack
W6 -1-03-019-001-1885
Mary Queen of the Scots: Vo
3/07/2017 13:50:26

1885

Queen Mary stepped away from the dance floor and started walking towards a quiet area in the corner of the great hall, "Which I am sure you have already done in my name. You are one of the Lords of the Congregation, are you not?"

"I am," nodded James as he walked with the queen.

"A busy last two years for you. Oh, I know about the religious wars you and your friends waged all over Scotland. While in Paris I received the reports of the violence, the burned churches and killings. François and I were both there when King Henri received word from my mother asking for help restoring order after Perth fell. You started quite the international war, mon frère! Did you like having France and England fight over Scotland like that, as if this country were nothing more than a prized Christmas turkey to be carved up and devoured?"

James smirked shrewdly as they reached the quiet space, "I was never worried; I knew we would win the war and we did! Scotland is free from popery! The mass is abolished! The only problem we still have is … you!"

"So much for clan loyalty!" scoffed Mary. "How can you call yourself a Stewart and yet work against your own sister, the lawful ruler of this country?!"

"I did not strike against you, my queen, only the pope!"

"Tell that to the innocents who died on both sides," snarled Queen Mary.

"Martyrs of their faiths; is any death more noble? Archbishop Crammer was burned at the stake because our cousin Queen Mary sought revenge over his role in King Henry the Eighth's divorce from Catherine of Aragon and marriage to Anne Boleyn. Catholics have no right to say they are innocent in this! Your kind have killed many reformers!"

"And your friend, John Knox? I heard tales of a book he wrote not only criticizing my mother and Queen Mary of England, but claiming that no woman has the right to rule over any man on any matter! Is it true?"

"Yes," nodded James. "And there John and I disagree. Being a woman is not the problem to me; only being catholic. I fully support Queen Elizabeth's right to rule in England."

Queen Mary looked away, her temper still simmering, "Of course you do."

Lord James touched Mary's hand as only a son of a king dared to, "Mary!" The queen glared at him. James removed his hand, "Mary, I do not hate you. I actually want to help you."

"Then why did you do so much to destroy my throne?"

"I was not thinking about you or your throne, not directly. You were France; your mother was the one we all lived with. I was against her, the lawful wife of our father when my own mother was simply a mistress. You never really knew your mother, Mary; I knew her quite well. She was … a powerful force, very capable. Yes, we fought! Parliaments always fight their kings and queens, especially in Scotland! To expect it to be different is like expecting the lochs to become mountains and the mountains to become seas!"

"Odd; François and I faced no such opposition in Paris!"

"France lost its traditional way of life when the Romans conquered them; we were never conquered and always remained free and independent. Individual freedom is cherished in Scotland; no one may rule here except by the consent of the people!" countered Lord James. "In France kings do as they want; there is no system to counter royal power in France the way there is in Scotland—or England for that matter."

"What would you have me do then?"

"I would have you accept that while you were in France this country became protestant. I would have you work with your parliament and not against us. Scotland will never be catholic again nor will the mass ever be legal in churches."

"And what about my own faith? I suppose you expect me to convert—or be killed?"

"Conversion is preferable, yes. But as that is unlikely, it is perhaps best to simply keep your religion to yourself and not concern yourself with religion in Scotland as a whole."

"You cannot expect me to give up the mass, Lord James. That is at the core of my faith."

"A compromise for your majesty may be possible; I will see what I can do."

"One more thing, Lord James: William Maitland. I understand he is on perhaps too good of terms with Queen Elizabeth's advisor William Cecil. I have use for that. Send him to London to secure from Queen Elizabeth her promise that when she is dead, the throne of England belongs to me and my heirs," commanded Queen Mary.

    Lightning lit up the Edinburgh sky, its thunder booming as torrents of rain soaked the grounds of Holyrood Palace. Watching the storm from her throne room Queen Mary petted one of her spaniels, the dog's soft fur soothing the nerves of the queen. A book rested on her lap. Two ladies in waiting watched the queen to see how they might best serve her. The door opened. Lord James Stewart entered with a bow, "Your Majesty, John Knox is here as commanded."

    "He may enter."

    Bowing, James stepped fully into the room, John Knox only three steps behind him. Wearing rich black robes and a black hat that contrasted against his long grey beard, John appeared to be sober and pious, "You sent for me?"

    Queen Mary stood up, raising herself to her full height of five feet eleven inches in a time where most women stood only five feet tall. Mary's finger tapped on the cover of the book she held before opening it to a bookmarked page, "'For nature has in all beasts printed a certain mark of dominion in the male, and a certain subjection in the female, which they keep inviolate. For no man ever saw the lion make obedience, and stoop before the lioness; neither yet can it be proved that the hind takes the conducting of the herd amongst the harts.' Did you write these words?"

"I did," confirmed John Knox.

"Were you aware when you wrote this book that it would be published and read by others?"

"Of course! Why else write it?"

"You preached against my authority as queen and encouraged people to rebel against me. As a result of this book and your teachings you led people to take up arms against my throne, to commit treason using the name of God. What have you to say on this?"

"God must be worshipped in accord with the Holy Bible and only the Bible. Anything that is not written in the Bible is idolatry. I preached the word of God and encouraged people to put away the rituals and images of a corrupt church led by the Anti-Christ in Rome," clarified John Knox.

"But you did more than this. You said that women have no right to rule over men."

"My book attacked your cousin, Queen Mary of England."

"Your book attacked women in general," countered Queen Mary.

"It was nothing personal, Madam."

"Nothing personal? I am a woman and you said that God forbids women from ruling over men. You used words from the Bible to justify hate and violence and to encourage people to take up arms against their God-ordained ruler."

"Princes are merely humans; they are flawed, sinful, and often the most ignorant of all men in matters of the true religion. When a ruler sins it is the duty of good Christians to resist and obey the Word of God. Indeed, think of what would have happened if Daniel and his fellows had not resisted Nebuchadnezzar? Or if the children of Abraham had worshipped the religion of the pharaoh in Egypt?"

"None of these took up arms against their kings!"

"They resisted in the ways God allowed them to; the only reason why they did not take up arms was because God did not give them the way to do so."

"God commands subjects to obey their king or queen even as children are commanded to obey their parents."

"That does not apply if the parent is a danger to their safety!" asserted John Knox.

Furious Queen Mary glared at him, standing still for fifteen minutes.

Concerned, Lord James spoke low and close to her ear, "What offends you, Madam?"

Meeting James' eyes, Queen Mary sat down in her throne. One of her ladies in waiting poured a cup of French wine which she drank deeply. Finally she answered, her eyes fixed on the wine in her cup, "Well then my subjects will obey you and not me. You have given them permission to do whatever they want. And because they will not obey me, I am made their subject instead."

John Knox took a step towards the queen in her throne, "God forbid that ever I take upon me to command any to obey me, or yet to set subjects at liberty to do what pleases them! My wish is that both princes and subjects obey God. Think not Madam that wrong is done you, when you are willed to be subject to God. It is He that subjects peoples under princes, and causes obedience to be given unto them."

"My conscience is to uphold the church in Rome and none other. Whatever you say, whatever you teach, it is clear that the Roman way is the right way."

"It is no longer the ways of Scotland, Madam. We have swept away the idols and the man-made catholic mass."

"I will not give these up. My heart is clear on the matter," asserted Queen Mary.

A servant entered with a bow, "Your dinner is ready, Your Majesty."

Queen Mary rose, "You are dismissed, Sir. Leave me." Obeying, John Knox bowed and left.

Chapter Three: Queen Mary Must Remarry

Two years passed. Celebrating the catholic mass privately in Holyrood, Queen Mary found herself enjoying a peaceful reign built on compromise: as long as she worshipped in private no one in her parliament at Edinburgh Castle would interfere in her personal religious affairs. Even John Knox seemed tamed; his attempts to deny Mary her religious freedom during one particularly violent incident now turning the Lords of the Congregation against him. The nobility, not the mob must rule Scotland decided her parliament.

For her part, Mary was content to compromise. Just as her cousin Queen Elizabeth asserted in England, Mary maintained a position that each subject in her realm was free to decide matters of religion for her or himself without interference from her government. This policy, along with her efforts to strengthen the monarchy at the expense of individual nobles made her very popular. She was the people's queen, likeable and easy to love by all but the nobility. Her happy and charming personality kept Scotland at peace with England, France, and Spain—without formal treaties or alliances.

It was a quiet, popular, and very effective reign. She was loved by even her greatest protestant critics, making friends where most nobles and royals tended to make enemies. She even achieved what seemed impossible: making her court more beautiful and glamourous like her court in France while also being accessible to commoners. No queen, not even her cousin Elizabeth, was loved more.

As a reward for his service in establishing a peaceful relationship with her parliament Queen Mary made Lord James Stewart the Earl of Moray and the Earl of Mar, an elevated status giving him more lands and income. But peace was not to last. She was childless and a widow. To secure the future of Scotland she needed to remarry and bear a son. Like her great uncle King Henry the Eighth before her this quest proved her undoing, changing Scotland in ways we still feel today.

"All hail to the days that merit more praise than all the rest of the year. And welcome the nights that double delights as well for the poor as the peer! Good fortune attend each merry man's friend. That doth but the best he may. Forgetting old wrongs with carols and songs to drive the cold winter away!" sang Queen Mary as she played her lute in her private apartment in Holyrood. Looking out the window she watched the snow dance from the sky to the ground. Now spending her fourth winter in Scotland since her return Mary found herself thankful for the many tapestries on the walls, each of them designed to make the room warmer by insulating from the cold Edinburgh winter storms.

Finally at length Mary put down her lute and approached Mary Seton, "The snow is so beautiful right now and my heart is merry. I am going outside for a walk and some exercise. Please bring me my furs and my boots."

Smiling Mary Seton went to the queen's closet for the requested clothes, "Do you wish to go hunt? Shall I send for the royal falconer?"

"No; I think I prefer to practice with my bow for a bit. No need for a large retinue. I only want some nice air and the peace to enjoy the snow."

Thirty minutes later Queen Mary strode into the newly fallen snow. Walking just twenty metres from the palace she observed archery targets already set up for her along with several quivers of arrows. Stringing her bow expertly she notched her first arrow into the string and sighted it to the center of the nearest target just thirty paces away. With a thump the arrow leapt from her bow to land solidly just three inches from the centre of the target. Picking up another arrow she aimed again. This time it landed in the centre.

"May I join you?" asked John Knox coming up from behind her.

"You may," affirmed Queen Mary as she sighted at a target placed forty paces away and shaped like a deer.

"Are you still resolved not to marry Robert Dudley?"

"Do you really think that offer was serious? It is clear to me that Robert Dudley no more wants me than I him. He loves Queen Elizabeth too much to ever leave her side. As far as I am concerned, it is well and good that he should stay in Whitehall with her and leave my Scotland alone."

"If not Dudley then, whose hand are you considering?" asked Knox as he aimed and fired at the target placed eighty paces away. The arrow thudded into the ground three metres short of the target.

"I was considering Don Carlos of Spain."

"You are not? He is after all one of the most eligible of men in all of Europe—and a Catholic."

"He is ugly, ill-tempered, violent, and sickly."

"Beggars cannot be choosers …"

"I am queen of Scotland; I am no beggar."

"Can you think of anyone else sufficiently royal who is not already married?"

"My cousin Henry Stewart Lord Darnley might be a suitable match. I hear he is quite handsome and tall like I am. Perhaps more importantly, he is of the blood royal for both England and Scotland just as I am."

"I have heard reports of him. Be careful your majesty; he might not be your type."

"Send for him, John. I will meet this Lord Darnley and see for myself."

Holyrood palace filled with music. Dancing Bransle les Lavandieres Queen Mary laughed as she clapped her hands during the four steps to the left. During the dance's following four steps to the right she put her hands into fists which she moved up and down as if rubbing a shirt against a washboard before turning in place in a circle over her left shoulder. Following the music's repeat Queen Mary stepped two steps to the left and two steps to the right. A tall and handsome nobleman entered the hall, approaching the circle of dancing couples who now repeated the bransle set. As Mary Seton prepared to step into the circle as the queen's dancing partner, the young man cut in, "May I?"

Mary Seton nodded and stepped out, allowing the man to take her place, shaking his finger at the queen as he stepped side to side. Following the music, the queen repeated the mimed scolding before stepping back into place to take the four steps to the left accompanied by clapping and the four steps to the right miming the wash board as the gentleman's partner. Two more repeats of the entire dance followed before the musicians played the final held note signalling all dancers to bow or curtsy. Politely the dancers applauded. Queen Mary turned to her new dancing partner, "Do I know you?"

The man bowed deeply, "No Your Majesty, not exactly."

"It is a bold thing to cut into a dance like that—particularly to dance with a queen."

"I am known for my boldness—and my exceptional good looks," laughed the man proudly.

"Who are you?"

"Henry Stewart, at Your Majesty's service!" smiled Henry proudly.

"You are Lord Darnley?"

"I am."

"You seem oddly familiar; did we meet before?"

Henry took the queen's hand and kissed it, "Once, in Paris. My mother sent me to express our sympathy for the loss of your father-in-law. You invited me to your coronation as queen of France."

"A lifetime ago it seems."

"Did you love your husband? He was quite the sickly fellow—not particularly handsome I might add. He seemed …what is the right word here…*undeserving* of your beauty and grace."

"And I suppose you feel yourself his better in these things?"

"Would you like me to show you? I am confident I can offer you proper evidence on this matter—in private of course."

Queen Mary laughed uncomfortably at his boldness, "I suppose you have practice in this matter whose fruits you offer me now?"

"Only you can be the judge of that," hinted Lord Darnley. As if on cue the musicians started the musical introduction to a galliard. Darnley put his arms around the queen as if for a lavolta section of the dance, "Dance with me!" Caught off guard Queen Mary found herself unable to speak, but nodded her consent. Boldly Henry took her hand, guiding her around the dance floor in the vigorous and very athletic dance filled with leaps, spins, kicks, and courtly flirting that took her breath away. When at last the dance finished, Darnley pulled her close to him, "Marry me!"

"Yes!" replied the queen, still breathless from the dance.

Gently Henry kissed her romantically. Queen Mary returned the kiss, her heart swept away.

"...I caution you this day that matrimony is a holy rite not to be entered into lightly or wantonly, to satisfy men's carnal lusts and appetites, like brute beasts that have no understanding. And so I charge thee: if either of ye knows a reason why ye may not lawfully marry, speak now! For most certainly ye will answer at the dreadful day of judgment when the secrets of all hearts shall be disclosed," preached Doctor John Sinclair, the bishop of Brechin, his eyes staring intensely at Lord Darnley despite the low light of the chapel royal in Holyrood Abbey. Confidently Henry met the bishop's eyes. After a full two minutes of waiting for Darnley to confess his sins in hopes of ending the wedding before the queen bound herself under God to Darnley, Doctor Sinclair found himself forced to continue, "Do ye Mary Stuart, queen of Scotland take this man Henry Stewart, Lord Darnley as your lawfully wedded husband? Do you promise to love, honour, and obey your husband, deferring to his wisdom in all things for as long as ye both shall live?"

Queen Mary held Henry's hands and met his eyes soberly, "I do."

The bishop turned to Lord Darnley, "Do ye Henry Stewart, Lord Darnley take this woman Mary Stuart, queen of Scotland as your lawfully wedding wife? Do you promise to love, honour, and cherish her as Christ loved the Church for as long as ye both shall live?"

"I do," answered Henry.

"By the power vested in me by the Church of Scotland I now declare ye husband and wife. You may kiss the bride," finished Doctor Sinclair. His trophy now secured, Henry kissed the queen as the object he saw her to be.

Breaking the kiss, Mary eyed him angrily. Henri smiled at her darkly, "And now I will take my leave of you, Mary so that you may celebrate your mass as you seem to think you must."

"What kind of catholic are you Henry to depart before our wedding is fully completed?"

"A little late for you to ask that question, now isn't it? The contract is signed; the vows are now taken. You are my wife, Mary!"

Mary fell to her knees, her stomach suddenly sick. Clutching at the gold embroidery covering the edges of her black velvet over gown, she fought the fabric of her white brocade petticoat in an attempt to rise back to her feet. Henry laughed at her, forcing Doctor

Sinclair to help her rise. Pleased with himself, Henry left the chapel as Sinclair led her by the hand and continued the wedding service, "Let us pray, my queen! Ave Maria…"

Mary joined in the prayer, "…gratia plena, Dominus tecum. Benedicta tu in mulieribus, et benedictus fructus ventris tui, Jesus. Sancta Maria, Mater Dei, ora pro nobis peccatoribus, nunc et in hora mortis nostrae. Amen."

"Ángele Dei, qui custos es mei, me, tibi commíssum pietáte supérna, illúmina, custódi, rege et gubérna. Amen," prayed Queen Mary in the chapel royal in Holyrood. Finishing her prayers she rose. Looking out the stained glass windows she noticed several leaves falling gracefully from the nearby trees. Loving the outdoors, her heart soared. Confidently she strode out of the chapel and towards her royal mews.

Henry intercepted her as if waiting just outside the chapel doors for her to leave, "Where do you think you are going?"

"Hunting; it is a fine cool day; perfect for hawking."

"You are not going anywhere," asserted Henry. "You are pregnant; you will behave yourself and obey me in the interests of our child."

"No woman miscarried by going hunting, least of all so early!" protested Queen Mary.

Henry raised his hand and slapped her hard against the face, "You will obey me!"

"Is this how you expect to gain the crown matrimonial from me, Henry? By beating me half to death before going to the bed of whoever will take you? I am queen of Scotland; I know what you do when you are not in my company!"

"You are only a woman!" laughed Henry. "You will give me what I want!"

"And if I refuse?"

"I will let the nobles do what they want of you. A catholic queen in a protestant country? You don't stand a chance!"

"Kill me and you will still not be king in your own right!" asserted Queen Mary.

"After you I have the next best claim to the thrones of both England and Scotland. So really, you have no choice but to obey me!"

Before Henry could hit her again, the queen's chief advisor and secretary, David Riccio walked down the hallway and spotted the queen, "Madam! You are bleeding!" Reaching the queen's side, the Italian glared at Henry, "Monstrum es, domine mi! Only a monster dares lays a hand of violence against his wife, let alone his sovereign queen!"

Henry mocked Riccio, "And to think you used to be my friend!"

"We were friends, Henry. But that was before you took to beating your wife. God forbid any man from reaching heaven who does such things!"

"I do not see why you are so protective, David. Mary's only a woman—and one sworn to obey me."

"Over my dead body!" cried Rizzio.

Henry smiled smugly, "I think I can arrange that!"

Chapter Four: Murder in Holyrood

Autumn yielded to winter. Encouraged by Secretary Rizzio, Queen Mary grew more and more independent of her nobles, preferring to make her own decisions instead of complying with policies that favoured corrupt nobles.

Upset at their loss of power and wealth, many protestant nobles spread rumours about the queen saying that Rizzio was her lover. These rumours attacked Darnley's vanity and gave him an excuse to become more violent, more abusive, and more hated by the queen.

As winter yielded to spring Darnley plotted with other enemies of the queen. Finally, in March the conspirators made their move.

"Sing for us, David!" laughed Queen Mary. Sitting at the head of her dining table in her private apartment, the queen drank deeply, her ladies in waiting and dearest friends Mary Seton, Mary Fleming, Mary Livingston, and

Mary Beaton enjoying the dinner party along with David Riccio.

"What song would you hear from me tonight?" asked David as he rose from the table to retrieve his lute from across the room.

"A bit from Goddesses, if you please!" requested Mary Seton.

"Excellent choice!" smiled David as he played the chorus as an instrumental introduction before singing the first two verses. "A north-country lass up to London did pass, although with her nature it did not agree. Which made her repent and so often lament, still wishing again in the north for to be. Oh the oak the ash, and the bonny ivy tree doth flourish at home in my own country. Oh the oak the ash, and the bonny ivy tree doth flourish at home in my own country.

"Fain would I be in the north country where the lads and the lasses are making of hay. There should I see what is pleasant to me: a mischief light on them entic'd me away. Oh the oak the ash, and the bonny ivy tree doth flourish most bravely in our country! Oh the oak the ash, and the bonny ivy tree doth flourish most bravely in our country!"

"Bravo! Ben cantato. La tua voce è come gli angeli in cielo!" applauded Queen Mary in Italian as David put down his lute.

"Vostra Maestà è troppo gentile," replied Riccio in Italian with a kiss to Queen Mary's hand.

Just then ten Scottish nobles burst into the room with drawn swords, their leader Henry Stewart strutting behind them with a drawn pistol in his hand. Henry motioned to Mary Seton, Mary Fleming, Mary Livingston, and Mary Beaton, "Leave or die!"

"What will you do?" screamed with horror Mary Seton as the men shoved her out of the room.

"None of your concern," snarled Henry as he grabbed his wife and pinned her against a wall, his pistol aimed and pointed at their unborn child. In full sight of the queen the nobles surrounded David Riccio with blades drawn.

Horrified Queen Mary was forced to watch as the nobles stabbed Riccio repeatedly, even after he was clearly dead. Crying, screaming, weeping, the queen's body shook uncontrollably in horror, "WHY?!"

"You will give me the crown matrimonial and make me king of Scotland in my own right!"

"NEVER!" screamed the queen.

"You will! When the child inside you dies this night; I promise you: you will give me what I want!" shrieked Henry as he turned and left her alone.

The next morning Queen Mary woke to find her bed surrounded by armed guards. Overnight Riccio's body was removed, leaving only his blood to testify to his murder. Pulling on a robe to cover herself the queen glared at the guards, "What is the meaning of this?"

"By order of parliament you are arrested," snapped one guard.

"And you are here to take me to my cell?" asked the queen shrewdly.

"No, Madam."

"Then how am I arrested?"

"You shall not leave Holyrood Palace nor walk its grounds without an armed guard to watch you at all times," declared the guard.

"I demand the earl of Moray brought to my presence," commanded Queen Mary. "Meanwhile am I free to walk my own house?"

"Yes Madam."

"Then leave my room and restore my ladies to me."

Stiffly the guards turned and left the queen alone.

Two days later Queen Mary received James Stewart in her throne room, her favourite spaniel wagging her tail happily at the sight of the queen's brother, "What is the meaning of this house arrest, James?"

"Parliament is filled with rumours, my queen."

"Parliament is always filled with rumours."

"Some say your husband murdered Secretary Riccio out of jealousy; that he was in fact far more to you than friend and advisor."

"Surely you know not to listen to this, especially given that half the women in Edinburgh have taken to his bed! If I were guilty of this sin—and you know I am not—I would be justified in doing so."

"The rules apply differently to women as to men," reminded James.

"I do not accept that, James. I am no less a queen than my father was king. If anything I have proven myself calm, just, and far more popular with the populace. Only the nobles dislike me and that more because I dare to actually rule as my own person. Even John Knox favours my company when hunting. I am truly amiable!"

"Nonetheless the nobles perceive you as less a ruler because you are a woman. Therefore to them you are guilty of adultery and conspired with your husband to murder Riccio."

"What illogical, self-serving rubbish!"

"You are heavily pregnant, Madam. Perhaps this is for the best," suggested James.

"James—you know this was Henry's idea. He wants the crown matrimonial and he doesn't care if he has to walk over my dead body or if he has to kill his own child to get it. What is worse: I really do not think he wants the power for its own sake. He likes it when people bow down to him and flatter him and seek his advice. He likes the fine clothes and ceremonies, the trappings of kingship but none of its responsibilities. Since my return to Scotland I have proven myself time and time again to be one of the most able and best liked of this dynasty! I am bright, educated, and very talented. I care about my people and uphold their liberties. I am a good queen! Why does my parliament not see it?"

"Mary—I know you, I know you speak the truth. But the greater political reality is that men rule the world and have no interest in giving up any of their powers and privileges in favour of women—not even a queen as talented, intelligent, and beautiful as you!"

One month later Henry Stewart received a personal note on his desk written by the queen, "Come to my chambers tonight for dinner." Surprised Henry smiled, "At last she comes to her senses!"

Two hours passed. A knock sounded at Queen Mary's door. Mary Livingston opened the door to admit Henry who was dressed in a gold doublet and black hose. Queen Mary rose from her table and greeted him with a passionate kiss, "You look so handsome! Were you ever this handsome before we married?"

Henry kissed her back, "Always—and more so. I did not dress to impress you that night, you know."

Mary laughed shrewdly, "Of course not."

"You have not asked me to dine for a long time."

"I have not been well. I fear for the baby, Henry."

"Oh?"

"Surely you do not want to hear of that! I cannot bear to have you worried!"

Henry helped her sit down at the table, "When it comes to our son, I would rather be worried."

Mary watched him sit down beside her, "Do you care for our son, Henry?"

"What father does not?"

"Do you want what is best for him?"

"Naturally!"

"Even if it not what the nobles want?"

"Nothing is too good for our son!"

Smiling in her heart, Queen Mary pouted, "The surroundings are too dull, Henry! Would you bear for our son to be born in this cage, even a gilded cage?"

"You tire of Holyrood?"

"I do not tire of it, my lord…but our son does! He's been sickly inside me. I can feel it! Please, if you have any compassion or fatherly love, will you not offer him a better place to be born?"

"What do you have in mind?"

"Edinburgh Castle—the palace is close to the Great Hall where Parliament meets—it is a better place—for all of us. You … me … and our little prince…."

"You want my help leaving Holyrood," concluded Henry.

"I am but a woman, my lord! What can I do but speak for our son?"

Henry smiled at her, impressed with her intelligent play of him, "Very well, I will give you what you want in exchange for spending the night in your bed doing whatever I want. No protests, just an obedient wife. Are we agreed?"

Mary smiled back, "I am your humble servant."

Two months later all of Scotland rejoiced. Bells rang in every village, every borough, every town, and every city celebrating the birth of the new prince on the nineteenth of June fifteen sixty six. Nowhere greater was the celebration than in Edinburgh Castle itself. From her office in the castle Queen Mary proudly wrote to her cousin Queen Elizabeth of her triumph. The boy was healthy! What more could she want?

That December Queen Mary and Lord Darnley celebrated their son's baptism at the chapel royal in Stirling Castle, naming him Prince James Stuart. Following royal custom, Prince James received Stirling Castle as his own house, removing him from both his parents' care. With James now safe in Stirling, Queen Mary attended to her own situation: ending the tyranny and abuse of her murderous husband.

Chapter Five: Loss of the Throne

"Are you sure you want to do this?" asked James Hepburn, the Earl of Bothwell from a quiet tavern table in Edinburgh.

Slightly disguised to conceal her identity from prying eyes Queen Mary nodded, "Yes, James! My husband must die. It is intolerable for any king or queen to be treated so cruelly."

"If I did not love you so much, I do not think I would risk so brash a plan."

"But you love me and you love Scotland. Darnley still demands I make him king in his own right. I cannot do that!"

"Nor should you; we have a lawful heir to the throne. Prince James is a fine boy already, even from the cradle.

"I was a cradle queen, you recall."

Bothwell smiled, "Yes you were and now look at you! Despite marriage, childbirth, and abuse you still shine as beautifully as you did at the moment of your return to Scotland."

Mary leaned in for a kiss, "It pleases me to hear you say that."

Bothwell kissed her, "I am forever at your service!"

February fifteen sixty seven dawned. In Glasgow Lord Darnley laid confined to his bed with sores that would not heal. Outwardly concerned for his health, Queen Mary travelled to Glasgow herself to check on him and retrieve him back to Edinburgh. Placing him in an Edinburgh house known as Kirk o' Field, Mary returned to Holyrood to personally supervise over the final details for a masque held in the honour of a friend. At last all was ready, filling Holyrood with music, dancing, drinking, and much laughter. Comedic theatre troupes performed for the guests. Jugglers, acrobats, and slight-of-hand magicians amazed the crowd. Happy, the queen went to her bed even as thunder—or what sounded like thunder—rolled through Edinburgh.

Dawn came. As constables rode out to investigate the source of the "thunder" they found Kirk o' Field completely blown apart with barely one stone left upon another. All that survived the blast was the garden. There, among the green grass and next to a pear tree lay Lord Darnley, his body untouched by burns and clearly murdered by strangulation. Immediately posters appeared across Edinburgh showing the queen as a seductive mermaid. In Parliament rumours spread that James Hepburn murdered Darnley. As the queen observed her forty days of official mourning for Darnley, the rumours grew louder and stronger. Finally as March flowed into late April Queen Mary had enough of Edinburgh for a while and journeyed forty miles north and west to Stirling Castle to visit the one Scot she knew loved her unconditionally.

"Alas my love you do me wrong to cast me off discourteously. For I have loved you oh so long delighting in your company. Greensleeves was all my joy and oh Greensleeves as my delight. Greensleeves my heart of gold and all for lady Greensleeves," sang Queen Mary as she snuggled Prince James tenderly. Smiling James cooed at his mother, bringing a smile to her face as she rocked him back and forth in her arms. "You are such a proper prince, you know that! Yes you are! And someday you are going to be king of Scotland and king of England too! Mummy promises because mummy knows you are a very good boy and will be a very good king!

"You know what James? I have a secret to tell you! Did you know I became queen when I was even younger than you! I lost my father when I was baby too! But your grandfather King James, he was a good king who died fighting the English. He was much nicer than your father who was very mean. You wouldn't like him. You are a good boy and will stay good forever, right?" James yawned. Sadly, Queen Mary put him back in his cradle to let him rest.

As she left the nursery James Hepburn intercepted her, "Time to go."

"Go? Go where?"

"Holyrood Abbey."

"Why would I go there, least of all with you?"

"To marry me, of course!"

"What makes you think I want to marry you?"

James held out a letter signed by several nobles, "Because your nobles command it."

"What?"

"I am your chosen consort. You will proceed with me to Holyrood to be married," commanded Bothwell.

"And if I do not?"

"Do you think Prince James can defend himself against an armed attack, even here? As a mother, do you want to risk it?"

"So this is how it is to be then? I submit to you in exchange for leaving my son alone?"

"Do you really want to risk losing Prince James in favour of the child you are bearing me? Yes, I know about your pregnancy; your ladies will talk given the right incentive to do so," hinted Bothwell darkly.

Furious Mary stood still, weighing her choices carefully. What would happen to Scotland if Prince James was murdered? Would Scotland itself survive or would it be conquered by England at last? Loving her country and loving her son even more, Queen Mary felt her hand in this forced, "I will obey."

Obedience did not save Queen Mary. Less than two months after her forced marriage to James Hepburn the nobles forced Queen Mary to abdicate her throne in favour of her son James. Imprisoned in Lockleven Castle, Mary was forced to watch and wait as nobles seized power in her son's name, the nobles finally naming her brother James Stewart as regent over his nephew.

As James' grand coronation as King James the Sixth carried on without her, Queen Mary felt a sharp pain. Summoning for a midwife she knew what had happened even before her ladies could tell her: the babies inside her were both dead, miscarried under the strain of the violence and death the year brought to her life. Weeping, Mary felt the strength of her mind weaken. Despair seized her. What more could she lose?

In answer to her prayer a stranger released her from her jail in Lockleven after ten months. Wars to regain her crown were fought by those still loving the young and beautiful queen. In defeat Queen Mary fled to England where she thought her cousin Elizabeth would come to her aide to restore her to her Scottish throne.

She was wrong.

Nineteen years of imprisonment in England followed. Nineteen years of sorrow and pain. Until at last she fell victim to her own envy for Elizabeth's crown, falling into a trap made for her by English spymaster William Cecil. In

October fifteen eighty-six the nobles of England tried Queen Mary for treason against Queen Elizabeth, the verdict and sentence decided before the trial began. For weeks Queen Elizabeth debated, delaying the sentence of death. Until at last on the eighth of February fifteen eighty-seven Queen Mary stood proudly to face her death as the queen she was. Words of compassion she spoke that morning. Gifts she gave to all those who were kind to her. Beneath her black velvet gown she wore crimson, the colour of Catholic martyrs. She died that day with grace and charm. "In my end is my beginning," was her life-long motto. All those who hated her in life came to love her in death with memory warm and glowing.

And so with love conclude we this tale of love, of courage, of Scotland.

Timeline

1489 28th November; Margaret Tudor is born to King Henry VII and Queen Elizabeth of York

1503 Margaret Tudor marries King James IV of Scotland

1512 10th April; Margaret Tudor gives birth to James V of Scotland

1531 Royal mistress Margaret Erskine gives birth to her son by King James V, James Stewart.

1533 7th September; Queen Anne Boleyn gives birth to Princess Elizabeth.

1536 19th May; Anne Boleyn is beheaded on Tower Green.

1536 9th October; The Pilgrimage of Grace revolt against King Henry VIII's dissolution of the monasteries ravages Yorkshire.

1541 18th October; death of Margaret Tudor

1542 8th December; Princess Mary Stuart* is born to Scotland's King James V and his French wife Marie of Guise

1542 14th December; death of James V; Princess Mary becomes queen of Scotland.

1546 May; King Henry VIII offers one thousand pounds to those who murder Scottish patriot Cardinal Beaton.

1546 29th May; Cardinal Beaton murdered in St. Andrews Scotland. John Knox joins with the murderers after the killing and is sentenced to ten years in the French galleys.

1547 28 January; death of King Henry VIII of England

1548 July; Five year-old Queen Mary is sent to France to marry Prince Francis along with Scottish nobles Mary Fleming, Mary Seton, Mary Beaton, and Mary Livingstone who remain in her service for the rest of her life.

1553 6th July; King Edward VI of England dies

1553 10th July; Lady Jane Grey is declared queen of England. She reigns for just nine days

1553 1st October; coronation of Queen Mary I of England.

1554 12th February; Lady Jane Grey is beheaded for treason after her father Henry Grey leads a rebellion in her name against Queen Mary I of England.

1557 winter; a small group of Scottish nobles sign "The First Band of the Protestant Congregation of Scotland" which promises to convert Scotland to Protestantism. This group later becomes known as the "Lord of the Congregation of Christ." Serving as regent for her daughter, Marie of Guise initially responds with tolerance.

1558 John Knox publishes "The First Blast of the Trumpet against the Monstrous Regiment of Women."

1558 24th April; Mary Queen of Scots marries Prince François, the dauphin of France

1558 17th November; Elizabeth receives news of the death of her sister Queen Mary I and becomes queen of England.

1559 15th January; coronation of Queen Elizabeth in Westminster Abbey.

1559 25th January to 8 May 1559; The first parliament of Elizabeth's reign produces the Acts of Uniformity and Supremacy which restores Protestantism as the religion of England and replaces Roman Catholicism with the Church of England (previously dissolved by Queen Mary I).

1559 May; the Lords of the Congregation launches a violent attack on Roman Catholic churches in Perth following a fiery sermon by John Knox. Mary of Guise sends an army to Perth, but is forced to fall back to Dunbar. Violence spreads as the Lords of the Congregation march on Edinburgh, leaving a wake of destruction and violence in their path and supported by a fleet of ships from Queen Elizabeth of England.

1559 July; John Knox writes to Queen Elizabeth I of England in defence of his "The First Blast of the Trumpet against the Monstrous Regiment of Women" which asserts that no woman has the right to rule over men in God's eyes.

1559 King Henri II of France dies. Henry Stewart Lord Darnley is sent to Paris to offer his sympathy to Prince François and Queen Mary, meeting them for the very first time. The couple invites Darnley to their coronation as king and queen of France.

1560 June; Queen Mary's mother Marie of Guise dies at the age of 45. The Lords of the Congregation finally end the religious wars, enabling both the English fleet supporting the Protestants and the French fleet supporting Queen Mary and her mother to withdraw from Scotland.

1560 August; the Lords of the Congregation call the Reformation Parliament and dissolve all ties to Rome. The catholic mass is legally banned in Scotland.

1560 December; King Francis II dies of an ear infection, rendering Queen Mary a widow.

1561 14th August; At odds with her mother in law Catherine de Medici, Queen Mary leaves France for the port of Leith in Edinburgh. The journey takes five days in hostile waters.

1561 September; Queen Mary sends her secretary William Maitland to London to negotiate with Queen Elizabeth regarding Mary's claim to the English throne. Queen Mary elevates her half-brother James Stewart to Earl of Moray and Earl of Mar.

1561 autumn; Queen Mary hires bass singer David Riccio to join her chapel quartet for an initial salary of £65.

1564 December; Queen Mary elevates David Riccio to secretary. Under Riccio's influence Queen Mary grows more independent of her Scottish nobles, ruling by her own decisions instead of following the council of others.

1565 February; Lord Darnley arrives at Queen Mary's court at Holyrood.

1565 March; rumours circulate at court that Queen Mary has already married Lord Darnley

1565 July Queen Mary marries her cousin Henry Stewart, Lord Darnley, a grandson of Queen Margaret Tudor and King James IV.

1566 March; Lord Darnley participates in the murder of Queen Mary's secretary David Riccio. The nobles of Scotland imprison the queen.

1566 19th June; Queen Mary gives birth to her son James at Edinburgh Castle.

1566 December; Queen Mary's son James is baptised in the chapel royal at Stirling castle.

1567 February; Lord Darnley is murdered by strangulation by a group of Scottish nobles, including James Hepburn, the Earl of Bothwell.

1567 24th April; Queen Mary visits her son James at Stirling Castle. She would never see him again.

1567 15th May; Queen Mary marries James Hepburn on orders of the Scottish nobles. Queen Mary is taken prisoner and imprisoned at Lockleven Castle.

1567 July; Queen Mary is forced to abdicate in favour of her son James. Prince James is crowned King James VI.

1568 May; Queen Mary sets sail for England with expectations her cousin will help restore her to her throne in Scotland.

1569 November to 1570 20th February; "The Rising of the North" by noble Catholics seeks to overthrow Queen Elizabeth in favour of the deposed Queen Mary of Scotland.

1586 October; Queen Elizabeth puts Queen Mary on trial for conspiracy to kill her.
1587 8th February; Queen Mary is beheaded at Fotheringhay Castle in England.

*Note: Stuart is the French form of Stewart and was the spelling Queen Mary used across her entire life. Thus the Stewart and Stuart dynasties are the same dynasty despite some members of the family using the originally Scottish spelling and some using the French spelling.

Prayers in Latin and Their Translations

Signum Crucis/The Sign of the Cross

In nómine Patris et Fílii et Spíritus Sancti. Amen.

In the name of the Father and of the Son and of the Holy Spirit. Amen.

Ave Maria/Hail Mary

Ave Maria, gratia plena, Dominus tecum. Benedicta tu in mulieribus, et benedictus fructus ventris tui, Jesus. Sancta Maria, Mater Dei, ora pro nobis peccatoribus, nunc et in hora mortis nostrae. Amen.

Hail Mary, full of grace, the Lord is with thee! Blessed art thou among women, and blessed is the fruit of thy womb, Jesus. Holy Mary, Mother of God, pray for us sinners, now and at the hour of our death. Amen.

Angele Dei/Angel of God

Ángele Dei, qui custos es mei, me, tibi commíssum pietáte supérna, illúmina, custódi, rege et gubérna. Amen.

Angel of God, my guardian dear, to whom God's love commits me here, ever this day be at my side, to light and guard, to rule and guide. Amen.

Song Lyrics from Mary Queen of the Scots

Depairte, Depairte (Scottish, 1545)
Depairte, depairte, allace I most depairte.
From hir that hes my hairt
With hairt full soir;
Again's my in deid and can find no remeid,
I wait the pan's of deid can do no moir!

Drive the Cold Winter Away (16th century)
All hail to the days that merit more praise
Than all the rest of the year.
And welcome the nights that double delights
As well for the poor as the peer!
Good fortune attend each merry man's friend.
That doth but the best he may.
Forgetting old wrongs with carols and songs
To drive the cold winter away

Goddesses (John Playford)

Vs 1:

A north-country lass up to London did pass,
although with her nature it did not agree.
Which made her repent and so often lament, still
wishing again in the north for to be.

Oh the oak the ash, and the bonny ivy tree
Doth flourish most bravely in our country!
Oh the oak the ash, and the bonny ivy tree
Doth flourish most bravely in our country!

Vs 2.

Fain would I be in the north country where the
lads and the lasses are making of hay.
There should I see what is pleasant to me: a
mischief light on them entic'd me away.

Oh the oak the ash, and the bonny ivy tree
Doth flourish most bravely in our country!
Oh the oak the ash, and the bonny ivy tree
Doth flourish most bravely in our country!

<u>Greensleeves (Traditional)</u>
Alas my love you do me wrong
To cast me off discourteously.
For I have loved you oh so long
Delighting in your company.
Greensleeves was all my joy
And oh Greensleeves as my delight.
Greensleeves my heart of gold
And all for lady Greensleeves.

Suggested Reading

Mary, Queen of Scots

Mary, Queen of Scots
http://www.royal.gov.uk/historyofthemonarchy/scottish%20monarchs(400ad-1603)/thestewarts/maryqueenofscots.aspx

BBC History: Renaissance and Reformation, Mary Queen of Scots
http://www.bbc.co.uk/history/scottishhistory/renaissance/features_renaissance_mary.shtml

Biography: Mary Queen of Scots
http://www.biography.com/people/mary-queen-of-scots-9401343

Mary Queen of Scots Biography and Facts
http://englishhistory.net/tudor/relative/maryqosbiography.html

Mary Stuart, Queen of Scots (1542-1587)
http://departments.kings.edu/womens_history/marystuart.html

Mary Stuart: The Story
http://www.marie-stuart.co.uk/story.htm

Mary wedded Francis, Dauphin of France on April 24th, 1558
http://www.historytoday.com/richard-cavendish/marriage-mary-queen-scots

Mary Stuart: the Poet
http://www.marie-stuart.co.uk/poetry.htm

Mary, Queen of Scots: Biography, Facts, Portraits & Information
http://englishhistory.net/tudor/relative/mary-queen-of-scots/

Bonjour La France: The Valois Dynasty
http://www.bonjourlafrance.com/valois-dynasty.htm

Robert Dudley to Marry Mary Queen of Scots
http://www.elizabethfiles.com/robert-dudley-to-marry-mary-queen-of-scots/4338/

Mary Queen of Scots: What Happened to Her Ladies in Waiting?
http://www.historyextra.com/article/stuart/mary-queen-scots-what-happened-her-ladies-waiting

Scottish Protestant Reformers

The First Blast of the Trumpet against the Monstrous Regiment of Women
http://www.swrb.com/newslett/actualNLs/firblast.htm

Lord of the Congregation
http://www.educationscotland.gov.uk/scotlandshistory/renaissancereformation/lordsofthecongregation/index.asp

William Maitland of Lethington
http://www.maryqueenofscots.net/people/william-maitland-lethington/

Cardinal David Beaton
http://www.undiscoveredscotland.co.uk/usbiography/b/cardinalbeaton.html

Cardinal Beaton Murdered
http://www.christianity.com/church/church-history/timeline/1501-1600/cardinal-beaton-murdered-11629972.html

July 1559. John Knox's Declaration to Queen Elizabeth
http://biblehub.com/library/knox/the_first_blast_of_the_trumpet/20_july_1559_john_knoxs.htm

BBC History: Renaissance and Reformation, Reformation II
http://www.bbc.co.uk/history/scottishhistory/renaissance/features_renaissance_reformation2.shtml

John Knox Interview with Mary Queen of Scots
http://www.reformation.org/john-knox-interview.html

Henry Stewart Lord Darnley

Lord Darnley
http://www.educationscotland.gov.uk/scotlandshistory/renaissancereformation/lorddarnley/index.asp

Luminarium: Lord Darnley
http://www.luminarium.org/encyclopedia/darnley.htm

BBC: Lord Darnley
http://www.bbc.co.uk/scotland/education/int/hist/mary/factfile/index.shtml?factfile=biog_darnley

Mary Queen of Scots.net: Lord Darnley
http://www.maryqueenofscots.net/people/henry-stuart-lord-darnley/

Murder of Darnley
http://www.educationscotland.gov.uk/scotlandshistory/renaissancereformation/murderofdarnley/index.asp

Mary's husbands
http://www.marie-stuart.co.uk/husbands.htm

David Riccio
http://www.luminarium.org/encyclopedia/rizzio.htm

British Heritage: the Murder of Lord Darnley
http://britishheritage.com/the-murder-of-lord-darnley/

The Ridolfi Plot –1571
http://www.gunpowder-plot.org/ridolfi.asp

Mary Queen of Scots Miscarriage Points to Collusion in Death of Lord Darnley
http://historymedmysteries.blogspot.com/2008/04/mary-queen-of-scots-miscarriage-points.html

Scotland

Edinburgh Castle
http://www.edinburghcastle.gov.uk/
Did You Know? Scotland's Cities
http://www.rampantscotland.com/know/blknow_cities.htm

The Tudor Dynasty

The Pilgrimage of Grace
http://www.historylearningsite.co.uk/pilgrimage_grace.htm

"Loving of my Husband," Jane and Guildford Dudley
https://allthingsrobertdudley.wordpress.com/2012/02/01/loving-of-my-husband-jane-and-guildford-dudley/

Lady Jane Grey (1537-1554)
http://www.bbc.co.uk/history/historic_figures/grey_lady_jane.shtml

The Rising of the North
http://www.tudorplace.com.ar/Documents/NorthernRebellion.htm

Elizabeth I, Parliament, Church, and Economy
http://faculty.history.wisc.edu/sommerville/361/361-16.htm

Chronology Part One: 1533-1569
http://www.elizabethi.org/contents/chronology/one.html

Chronology Part Two: 1570-1603
http://www.elizabethi.org/contents/chronology/two.html

Food, Religion, and Culture

Medieval Food and Cooking
http://www.castlesandmanorhouses.com/life_04_food.htm

Latin Prayers
http://www.adoremus.org/Latin-Prayers.html

Fish Eaters – Prayers
https://fisheaters.com/prayers.html

Historical Perspectives on Falconry
http://www.antithetical.org/restlesswind/plinth/falconry2.html

Whitehall Palace and Court
http://www.british-history.ac.uk/survey-london/vol13/pt2/pp41-115

Whitehall Palace
http://www.everycastle.com/Whitehall-Palace.html

French Medieval Desserts (recipe site)
http://www.justapinch.com/recipes/dessert/other-dessert/french-medieval-desserts.html

All Gode Cookery Recipes: Desserts and Sweets
http://www.godecookery.com/allrec/allrec04.htm

A Brief History of Desserts and Puddings
http://www.localhistories.org/desserts.html

Recipes: the Stuart Age
http://www.celtnet.org.uk/recipes/stuart-recipes.php

Music and Dance

Heart's Ease (Dance steps)
http://www.pbm.com/~lindahl/dance/Hearts_Ease.html

Drive the Cold Winter Away
Hymns and Carols of Christmas: Drive the Cold Winter Away

Drive the Cold Winter Away
http://www.hymnsandcarolsofchristmas.com/Hymns_and_Carols/drive_the_cold_winter_away.htm

What are Playford Dances?
https://round.soc.srcf.net/playford

Bransles
http://www.pbm.com/~lindahl/del/sections/bransles.html

Songs of and About Elizabethan Times
http://www.renfaire.com/Language/songs.html

Elizabethan Songs
http://www.elizabethan-era.org.uk/elizabethan-songs.htm

Facsimile of John Playford's "The English Dancing Master"
http://www.pbm.com/~lindahl/playford_1651/
Belle Qui Tiens Ma Vie—English Translation
http://www.users.on.net/~algernon/bellequitiens/translation.html

Dances of France and Burgundy
http://www.pbm.com/~lindahl/del/sections/dances_from_france_and_burgundy.html

Pennsic Pile: Sheet Music for Dances
http://www.cs.cmu.edu/~kvs/music/pile/pieces.html

SCA Renaissance Dance Homepage
http://www.pbm.com/~lindahl/dance.html

Printed in Great Britain
by Amazon